Question Time

Mammals

Jim Bruce

Editor: Emma Wild
Designer: Catherine Goldsmith
DTP Co-ordinator: Nicky Studdart
Consultants: Joyce Pope, Norah Granger
Indexer: Sue Lightfoot
Production controllers: Jacquie Horner, Caroline Hansell
Illustrators: Ruth Lindsay 8–9, 14–15, 22–23; **Lisa Alderson**
12–13, 18–19; **Robin Budden** 26–27.
Cartoons: Ian Dicks
Picture manager: Jane Lambert
Picture acknowledgements: 7cr Ingrid N. Visser/Planet Earth
Pictures; **9**cl Michael Gogden/www.osf.uk.com; **17**tl Fritz
Polking/Still Pictures; **21**tr E A Janes/RSPCA Photo library;
27cr Images Colour Library.

Every effort has been made to trace the copyright holders of the photographs.
The publishers apologise for any inconvenience caused.

KINGFISHER
Kingfisher Publications Plc,
New Penderel House,
283–288 High Holborn,
London WC1V 7HZ
www.kingfisherpub.com

First published by Kingfisher Publications Plc 2001
10 9 8 7 6 5 4 3 2 1

1TR/1200/TIM/RNB/MA128

A CIP catalogue record for this book
is available from the British Library.

ISBN 0-7534-0626-8

Printed in China

CONTENTS

ABOUT this book

Have you ever wondered what a kangaroo keeps in its pouch? On every page, find out the answers to questions like this and other fascinating facts about mammals. Words in **bold** are explained in the glossary on page 31.

Look and find
dragonfly

All through the book, you will see the **Look and find** symbol. This has the name and picture of a small object that is hidden somewhere on the page. Look carefully to see if you can find it.

Now I know...

★ This box contains quick answers to all of the questions.
★ They will help you remember all about the amazing world of mammals.

WHAT is a mammal?

Although mice, bats, giraffes, leopards and whales may seem very different, they all belong to a group of animals called mammals. Mammals are animals that have special things in common. They are **warm-blooded**, have fur or body hair, and have bony skeletons that support their bodies. Most mammals give birth to live young, and the mothers feed their young on their milk. All these things are true about us, so humans are mammals too.

Giraffes feeding and drinking

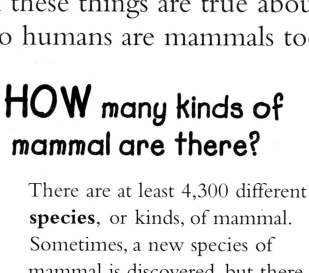

Mother leopard with cub

HOW many kinds of mammal are there?

There are at least 4,300 different **species**, or kinds, of mammal. Sometimes, a new species of mammal is discovered, but there are probably no more than a few new species left to be found.

Harvest mouse

That's Amazing!

Humans live longer than any other mammal – a few have lived for more than 120 years!

Mammals are the most intelligent of all the animals and have extra-large brains!

4

HOW big do mammals grow?

Mammals come in all shapes and sizes, from tiny to very large. About half of all known mammals are small **rodents**, such as squirrels and mice, and about one quarter are bats. Some mammals, such as elephants, whales and lions, grow to be very large. The sea-living blue whale is the biggest mammal of all, and weighs more than 150 tonnes. The largest land mammal is the African elephant, which can weigh up to eight tonnes.

Although human babies are bigger than many fully grown mammals, they are completely helpless. They need their parents to look after them for many years.

Now I know...

★ Mammals may look very different, but they have many things in common.

★ More than 4,300 different species of mammal exist.

★ Some mammals grow to be very large, but most are quite small.

5

HOW do polar bears keep warm?

Like all mammals, polar bears are warm-blooded animals. Their bodies stay at the same temperature whether the air or water around them is hot or cold. Most mammals are also covered in hair. Polar bears have a very thick coat to keep out the freezing cold of the **Arctic**. In winter, they also shelter in a **den**, or hole, which they dig in the snow.

WHY is a polar bear white?

As well as to keep it warm, a polar bear has a white coat to **camouflage** it against the snow when it hunts for food. In fact, its whole body is perfect for life in its surroundings. Its large paws are excellent snow-shoes as well as great paddles for swimming.

That's Amazing!

Polar bears do not need to drink. They get all their liquid from the food they eat!

Polar bears can swim for 100 km without stopping!

Polar bear

WHAT makes a walrus fat?

Under its skin, a walrus has a thick layer of fat called **blubber**. This keeps it warm in the icy waters of the Arctic. Other Arctic mammals, such as polar bears and seals, also have this layer of fat to protect them from the cold. A walrus has two long, sharp tusks, which it uses to dig up shellfish and crabs from the seabed. The tusks are also used as weapons when fighting.

To stay fat and warm, Arctic mammals must eat a lot of food. A polar bear eats seals, fish, seabirds and walruses, plus plants and berries in the summer. Polar bears have an amazing sense of smell. They can sniff out a live seal one metre under the ice.

Seal

Now I know...

★ All mammals are warm-blooded.
★ A polar bear's white coat camouflages it against the snow.
★ Blubber is a layer of fat under Arctic mammals' skin that keeps them warm.

WHERE do mammals live?

Mammals live almost everywhere in the world – in water as well as on land. Every sort of mammal has its own **habitat**. This is the place where it finds its food and spends most of its life. Mammals are found in places as different as dry deserts and wet forests, and from the hot tropics to the freezing polar regions.

WHAT does a camel keep in its hump?

Camels are well equipped for life in the hot, dry desert. They can survive for days without food and water. The humps on their backs are big stores of fat, which they can live off when they cannot find food.

Dromedary camels

That's Amazing!

When they cannot find food, camels have been known to eat rope, sandals and even tents!

Sloths don't clean their fur, so after a while it grows green slime, and beetles and moths come to live in it!

WHY is a sloth so lazy?

Sloths spend most of their lives hanging upside down in trees in their **rainforest** habitat in South America. Sloths eat only the leaves of plants that grow nearby, so some days they hardly move more than a few centimetres when looking for food. Staying still also helps them hide from their enemies.

A camel has a thick coat to protect it from the heat of the Sun. The pads on its feet protect against the hot sand. These pads also spread out and help the camel to walk on the loose sand.

Sidewinder snake

Now I know...

★ Mammals live in every part of the world – on land and in water.

★ Camels keep spare stores of fat in humps on their backs.

★ Sloths rarely move from their upside-down position.

WHY are whales such whoppers?

Larger than any dinosaur, the blue whale is the biggest animal that has ever lived. An adult can grow up to 33 metres long, the same length as a jumbo jet. It can weigh more than 150 tonnes, which is as heavy as 30 elephants. The blue whale is able to grow so huge because its giant body is always supported by the water around it. Whales are powerful swimmers. Some can even leap out of the water.

WHAT is a blowhole?

Sea-living mammals, such as whales and dolphins, cannot breathe underwater like fish. They must come to the surface for air. They breathe in and out through a **blowhole**. This is the nostril or breathing-hole on the top of the head. When they let out the used air, they send out a spray of water called a spout.

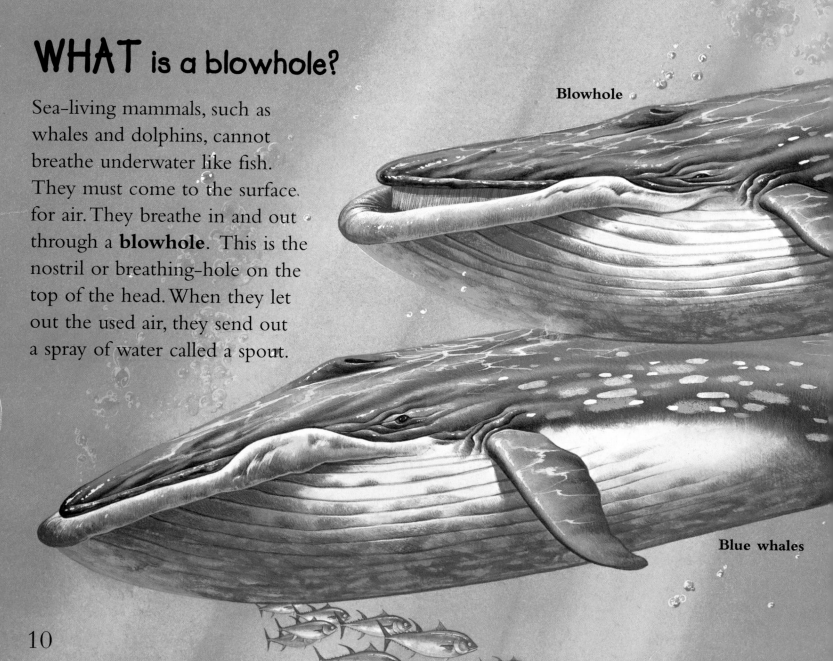

Blowhole

Blue whales

10

HOW do dolphins swim?

Dolphins are wonderful swimmers. Instead of hands and feet they have flippers and a tail. They swim by moving their tail up and down. Their smooth shape slips easily through the water.

That's Amazing!

Sailors have been known to mistake a whale for an island and try to land on it!

The sperm whale can hold its breath underwater for more than two hours!

Now I know...

★ Whales are the biggest animals in the world - ever.

★ Sea-living mammals must hold their breath underwater.

★ Dolphins swim using their flippers and tails to power along.

Blue whales use their mouths like sieves to strain krill, a tiny kind of shrimp, from the water.

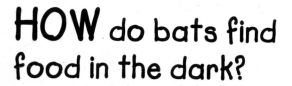
WHICH mammals can fly?

Bats are the only mammals that can truly fly. Like birds, they have light bodies, but they have no feathers. Their wings are layers of skin stretched between long finger bones. Bats are **nocturnal** and sleep during the day. They hang upside down from cave roofs or tree branches. As the Sun sets, they fly into the night in search of food.

Flying fox bat

HOW do bats find food in the dark?

Most bats have poor sight. While hunting at night, they send out high-pitched squeaks that bounce off objects and return to the bats' ears as echoes. This is called **echolocation**. From these sounds, the bats can tell where things are – such as tasty insects.

Kitti's hog-nosed bat

This minute bat is one of the world's smallest mammals. It is about the size of a bumble bee and weighs no more than 2 grammes.

That's Amazing!

One type of insect-eating bat can eat 600 mosquitoes in an hour!

Sometimes, millions of bats live together in a huge group called a colony!

WHY do sugar gliders leap from trees?

The Australian sugar glider leaps from the treetops to find food or to escape from enemies. Although it has no wings, it has a thin, furry skin that stretches along its body. This helps it to glide from tree to tree, like a paper dart. It can travel 50 metres in one jump.

Most bats are **insectivores** – they eat only insects. But some bats, such as the flying fox, feed on fruits.

Now I know...

★ Bats have wings and are the only mammals that can fly like birds.
★ Sugar gliders cannot fly. but glide from tree to tree.
★ Most bats hunt during the night using their excellent hearing.

WHAT do hippos eat?

Like many other mammals, the hippopotamus is a vegetarian and eats only plants. Mammal plant-eaters are called **herbivores**. They have strong teeth to help them grind up their tough food, and special stomachs to digest it. To get all the energy they need, they have to spend many hours every day feeding.

WHICH mammals chew and chew?

Hoofed mammals, such as buffaloes, giraffes and antelopes, feed mainly on grass and leaves. As their diet is so tough, they munch their food twice. After grabbing a big mouthful, they quickly swallow it after one chew. The food goes into their stomachs, but comes back up for a second chew after it has become softer.

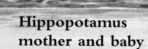

Elephants

Buffaloes

Hippopotamus mother and baby

A hippo bathing

Because they all eat a range of different foods, many plant-eaters can live in the same area. In the evening when the Sun has set, many herbivores go to the local waterhole to feed.

14

Giraffes eating acacia leaves

WHY do giraffes have long necks and legs?

The world's tallest mammal is the giraffe. It can be as tall as five metres. It gets its great height from its very long neck and legs. Being so tall, giraffes can stretch right up into the trees to pull off juicy leaves and shoots that other animals cannot reach. Even though its neck is long, a giraffe has only seven neck bones – the same number as all other mammals.

That's Amazing!

As well as being the tallest mammal, a giraffe also has a huge tongue – more than 45 cm in length!

Hippos are very large animals – no wonder – they eat about 60 kg of plants every day!

Antelope

Zebras drinking at a waterhole

Some mammals, such as humans, can eat plants and meat. They are called **omnivores**.

Now I know...

★ Many mammals, such as hippos and giraffes, are plant-eaters.
★ Herbivores chew their food over and over again.
★ Giraffes have long necks and legs, so they can reach treetops.

15

WHERE do lions catch their dinner?

Mammals that are meat-eaters, such as lions, tigers and cheetahs, are called **carnivores**. Big cats are built to hunt, and have powerful bodies, sharp eyesight and a good sense of smell. Lions live in family groups called **prides**. They hunt their **prey** on the plains and in the woodlands of Africa. The females of the group do most of the hunting, but the males soon arrive to make sure they get their share of the feast.

That's Amazing!

Cheetahs love making lots of noise - they are always chirping, purring, humming and yelping!

Unlike most cats, tigers are very fond of water, and are strong swimmers!

A lion can eat 23 kg of meat in one meal - that's the same as more than 250 beefburgers!

WHAT is the fastest mammal?

The cheetah is the fastest mammal. It can run at a top speed of 110 kilometres per hour, but only in short bursts. Unlike most cats, its claws stick out all the time, helping it to grip the ground as it runs.

Two lionesses chase an antelope

WHY do tigers have stripes?

Tigers are easy to recognize, with thick black stripes covering their orange body. These markings help them blend in with the light and shade of the forest. They can creep up quickly and quietly on their prey without being spotted, especially at sunset when they like to hunt.

Now I know...

★ Carnivores, such as the big hunting cats, eat only meat.
★ The fastest mammal in the world is the speedy cheetah.
★ A tiger's stripes help to keep it hidden in the forest.

HOW do beavers build their home?

Many mammals build homes to shelter their young. A whole beaver family helps to build a **lodge** in the river. This structure is made from logs, branches and rocks stuck together with mud. The beavers cut the logs by gnawing through trees with their sharp teeth. Inside the lodge is an area above water that is warm and dry even in bad weather. Here, the beavers can bring up their young in safety.

Beaver

WHY do dormice need a nest?

Dormice have nests to keep them snug and protected. During the cold winter, they spend several months asleep, or **hibernating**. The hibernating animal's body slows down and its heart beats less often. It does not eat and lives off fat stored in its body.

That's Amazing!

Beavers build canals more than 200 m long to make quick routes from one river to another!

More than 400 million prairie dogs lived in one underground town in Texas in the U.S.A.!

18

WHERE do prairie dogs live?

A prairie dog is a type of rodent living in North America. Family groups dig underground burrows. These are linked together by tunnels to make towns for hundreds of prairie dogs. Some act as sentries and keep watch above ground for enemies.

Lodge

Now I know...

★ Beavers live in wooden lodges on the river that are built by all the family.

★ In the winter, hibernating animals keep warm in nests.

★ Prairie dogs live in burrows that link to make vast towns.

WHERE do gorillas live together?

Gorillas are shy, gentle creatures that live in the remote forests of Central Africa. They travel in family groups, which include an adult male, several females and their babies. During the day, a group will move slowly through the forest, looking for food, and resting while the young play. Just before dark, the gorillas build their nests from branches and leaves, and curl up to sleep.

Look and find butterfly

WHO is leader of the pack?

Wolves, like many other mammals, live in family groups. They hunt together in packs which are led by a **dominant** male. When two wolves meet, they use body language to work out who is the boss.

Grey wolves in a pack

Silverback

That's Amazing!

A baby gorilla will ride 'piggyback' until it is almost three years old!

Despite what fairy stories say, wolves stay away from humans as much as possible!

WHY do zebras have stripes?

Zebras are famous for their stripes, but no one really knows why these African horses have them. It may be that the black-and-white pattern is a camouflage. Or it may help to keep the zebras cool in the hot sun. As no two zebras have exactly the same pattern, it is more likely that the stripes are like a signal, to help foals find their mothers in the large group.

Some male gorillas are called silverbacks. They get their name from the silver hairs that grow on their backs. These hairs appear when a male gorilla is about ten years old.

Now I know...

★ Gorillas live in family groups in the forests of Central Africa.
★ Often, groups of mammals are led by one male.
★ Zebras tell each other apart by the stripes on their bodies.

WHEN do elephants stop growing?

When they are born, most mammal babies are blind and helpless, but newborn elephant calves can walk when they are just one hour old. Unlike other young, they never completely stop growing. The older they get, the larger they grow. Female elephants will stay with their mothers and relatives in the same herd long after they become adults.

HOW do young mammals learn?

Mammals give their young more protection and training than other animals do. Young mammals learn many skills from their mothers, such as finding food and keeping out of danger. Sometimes, the father also cares for the young. He protects them from enemy attack, and helps to find food for them.

That's Amazing!

When it is born, a baby elephant weighs 145 kg – more than twice the weight of an adult human!

The Asian elephant is pregnant for 609 days – over two and a half times as long as a human!

WHAT do piglets eat?

For their first few weeks, a mother pig feeds her piglets on her milk. Mammals are the only animals that do this. Some mammals, such as elephants, feed milk to their young until they are several years old.

A young elephant is protected by the females in the herd

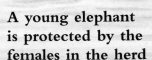

Elephants love bathing. They are very good swimmers, and can give themselves a shower by squirting water through their trunks.

Now I know...

★ Elephants are so huge because they do not stop growing – ever.
★ Mammal mothers teach their babies survival skills.
★ Piglets, like all mammals, feed on their mother's milk.

WHAT does a kangaroo keep in its pouch?

Kangaroos belong to a group of mammals called **marsupials**. Marsupial mothers have a pouch on the front of their stomachs. When a baby kangaroo, or joey, is born, it is only about 2 centimetres long. It is too tiny to survive in the outside world, so it crawls up into its mother's warm pouch. Once there, the baby drinks milk and grows bigger. After eight months, it is large enough to leave the pouch safely.

Like most marsupials, kangaroos are only found in the wild in Australia.

That's Amazing!

The leaves that koalas eat contain strong-smelling oils that keep bugs away!

A platypus finds food in the mud using special electric sensors inside its bill!

Female red kangaroo with her joey

24

WHY do koalas love to sleep and sleep?

Koalas are expert climbers, and spend most of their time in eucalyptus trees, eating the young shoots. Their leafy diet does not give them much energy, so they sleep for up to 18 hours a day. They only become active at night when it is time to eat again.

WHICH mammals lay leathery eggs?

Two mammals, the platypus and the echidna (a spiny anteater) do not give birth to live young. Instead, they lay eggs that are protected by leathery shells. After laying her eggs in a nest, the mother platypus warms them with her body for about ten days until they hatch. Mammals that lay eggs are called **monotremes**.

Now I know...

★ A female kangaroo has a pouch, so that her baby has a safe place to grow.

★ Koalas are lazy - they sleep for up to 18 hours every day.

★ The platypus and the echidna are the only mammals that lay eggs.

WHY do chimps chatter?

Almost all mammals have some way of **communicating** with animals of their own kind. Chimpanzees communicate, or 'chatter', using sounds and signs. They bark, pant or grunt, to tell others when food is found. They hoot loudly and beat on tree-trunks to warn when enemies are nearby. Chimps often greet each other with hugs and kisses, just like humans.

That's Amazing!

Scientists have found that chimps treat themselves for illness using plants from the forest as medicines!

Wild chimps use leaves as sponges to soak up water or to drink!

Young chimpanzee

WHAT does a dog's bark mean?

Dogs bark at other animals to tell them where their **territory** is. An animal's territory is the area that it moves around and where it feeds. A pet dog's territory may be around its owner's house. Dogs will also bark if they are excited, or just want to say 'hello'.

Sheep dog

WHICH mammals love to 'talk'?

Like other intelligent mammals, dolphins are playful and communicative. They live in groups called schools, and 'talk' to each other using clicks and whistles. These sounds travel under the water for many kilometres. Scientists also think that dolphins can copy human speech, but at a much faster rate.

A chimp communicates with its group

Chimps spend a lot of their time in trees. They use their strong arms to swing from branch to branch in search of food. At night, they build treetop nests from leaves and sleep in them.

Now I know...

★ Chimps send messages to each other using sounds and signs.

★ A dog's bark can mean 'hello' or 'keep away please!'.

★ Dolphins are intelligent and 'talk' to each other.

WHY are tigers in danger?

The tiger is one of the most **endangered** animals in the wild. For many years, thousands have been killed illegally by hunters for their fur and other body parts. In Asia, farmers have cut down the tigers' forest home to grow crops. To help these animals survive, special areas called **reserves** have been created for them, where hunting is banned. Many zoos have tried to breed tigers to release back into the wild.

WHO hunts rhinoceroses?

Every year, illegal hunters called poachers kill thousands of rhinoceroses for their horns. The horns are ground up and used in medicines because many people believe they can cure illnesses. Because of hunting, rhinos are the fastest-disappearing large mammals in the world.

White rhinoceros

That's Amazing!

A tiger's mighty roar can be heard more than 3 km away!

Rhino horn is made from keratin – the same material that your hair and nails are made from!

ROAR

HOW many pandas are left in the wild?

Fewer than 1,000 wild pandas still live in their natural home in the mountain forests of southern China. So few are left because they feed on a plant called bamboo, which is becoming rare in this area. Another problem is that pandas have only a few babies in their lifetime, and many of them die young.

Some sea mammals are also in danger of dying out. Although most whales and dolphins are protected, many of them are still killed every year.

Now I know...

★ Tigers are becoming rare – reserves are being set up to protect them.

★ Rhinos are hunted by poachers for their valuable horns.

★ Pandas are very rare – fewer than 1,000 are left in the wild.

MAMMAL QUIZ

What have you remembered about mammals? Test what you know and see how much you have learned.

1 What does a giant panda eat?
a) bamboo
b) grass
c) eucalyptus

2 Which mammal has blubber?
a) mouse
b) gorilla
c) walrus

3 Which mammal eats only plants?
a) giraffe
b) lion
c) polar bear

4 Which mammal lives in a lodge?
a) dolphin
b) koala
c) beaver

5 Which mammal has a pouch?
a) seal
b) bat
c) koala

6 Which mammal can fly?
a) sugar glider
b) bat
c) kangaroo

7 Which mammal is the fastest runner?
a) bat
b) whale
c) cheetah

8 Which sound does a dolphin make?
a) whistle
b) bark
c) roar

9 What is a camel's hump made of?
a) blubber
b) hair
c) fat

10 Where does a polar bear live?
a desert
b) Arctic
c) jungle

Find the answers on page 32.

GLOSSARY

Arctic The cold area around the North Pole.

blowhole The nostrils of a whale or dolphin, found on the top of the head.

blubber A thick layer of fat under a sea mammal's skin that keeps it warm.

camouflage A colour, shape or pattern that hides an object. A camouflaged animal looks just like its background, so it is hard to see.

carnivores Animals that eat mainly meat.

communicating The passing on of information, feelings and ideas.

den The hollow home of a wild animal.

dominant The most powerful animal in a group.

echolocation The system used by bats and dolphins to find their way in the dark.

endangered When a species is at risk of dying out.

habitat The natural home of an animal or plant.

herbivores Animals that eat only plants.

hibernating When animals spend several winter months in a deep sleep.

insectivores Animals that only eat minibeasts.

lodge A beaver's home, built from logs and rocks stuck together with mud.

marsupials Mammals, such as kangaroos and koalas, that bring up their young in pouches.

monotremes Mammals that lay eggs rather than giving birth to live young.

nocturnal Busy and active at night rather than during the day.

omnivores Animals that are both meat- and plant-eaters.

prey An animal that is hunted or killed by another animal.

prides Family groups of lions.

rainforest A dense forest with very heavy rainfall.

reserves Special areas where wild animals are protected from poachers, and the land is free from farming.

rodents Small mammals with large, sharp front teeth for gnawing.

species A particular type of animal or plant.

territory The area in which an animal lives and hunts.

warm-blooded Having a constant body temperature.

INDEX

Answers to the Mammals Quiz on page 30

★ 1 a ★ 2 c ★ 3 a ★ 4 c ★ 5 c ★ 6 b ★ 7 c ★ 8 a ★ 9 c ★ 10 b